MOTIVATIONAL QUOTES FOR CHANGE

HARNESSING THE POWER OF WORDS

DR. JAGADEESH PILLAI

Made with ♥ on the Notion Press Platform
www.notionpress.com

|| Dedicated to all wisdom seekers around the world ||

ജ

Contents

Contents

PRAYER

"Om Bhadram Karnebhih Shrunuyaama DevaahBhadram Pashyemaakshabhiryajatraah SthirairangaistushtuvaamsastanoobhihVyashema Devahitam YadaayuhSwasti Na Indro VridhashravaahSwasti Nah Pooshaa VishwavedaahSwasti Nastaarkshyo ArishtanemihSwasti No Brihaspatir DadhaatuOm Shantih, Shantih, Shantih"

The literal meaning of this mantra is: OM. O Gods! Let us hear auspicious words from our ears. O reverent Gods! Let us behold propitious visions from our eyes, let our organs and body be stable, healthy, and strong. Let us do that which is pleasing to the gods in the life span allotted to us. May Indra, inscribed in the scriptures, bring us fortune! May Pushan, the knower of the world, grant us prosperity! May Trakshya, who vanquishes enemies, bestow us with blessings! May Brihaspati bring us success!
OM Peace, Peace, Peace.

ABOUT THE AUTHOR

Dr. Jagadeesh Pillai is a renowned Guinness World Record holder, writer, and researcher hailing from Varanasi, also known as the abode of Lord Shiva. With a Ph.D. in Vedic Science and a range of creative ideas and achievements, he is a true polymath. He is the author of more than 100 books including Research Publications. Although his roots can be traced back to Kerala, the people of Varanasi hold him in high regard and affectionately consider him one of their own.

Dr. Pillai has achieved four Guinness World Records in the following subjects:

"Script to Screen" - In this record, Dr. Pillai produced and directed an animation film within the shortest time possible, breaking the previous record set by Canadians. He has also received numerous national and international awards and recognitions for this achievement.

Longest Line of Postcards - For this record, Dr. Pillai created a line of 16,300 postcards on the occasion of the 163rd anniversary of Indian Postal Day. The event also included a questionnaire about the Indian flag.

Largest Poster Awareness Campaign - Dr. Pillai designed an awareness campaign on the subject of "Beti Bachao - Beti Padhao" (Save the Girl Child - Educate the Girl Child) to achieve this record.

Largest Envelope - In tribute to the Indian Prime Minister's

"Make in India" initiative, Dr. Pillai created a 4000 square meter envelope using waste paper to achieve this record.

Attempted - **70000 Candles on a 210 kg Cake** - To celebrate the 70th Indian Independence Day, Dr. Pillai attempted to light 70,000 candles on a 210 kg cake, which was recorded in World Records India.

Attempted - **Documentary on Dhamek Stupa of Sarnath in 17 Languages** - Dr. Pillai attempted to create a documentary on the Dhamek Stupa of Sarnath, dubbing it in 17 different languages. The result of this attempt is currently awaiting confirmation from the Guinness World Records.

Dr. Pillai is skilled in teaching the Bhagavad Gita, a Hindu scripture, and is popular among young people. He has helped many young people improve their lives through his motivational teachings.

In addition to teaching, he has composed and sung numerous Sanskrit Bhajans and patriotic songs.

He has also written and directed several short films and documentaries for awareness campaigns, and has volunteered with the police in both UP and Kerala to spread awareness about various issues through videos and photography.

Incredibly, he has produced and directed over 100 documentaries about the city of Varanasi, all on his own.

He has also helped and guided more than 25 boys and girls to achieve world records through creative and innovative methods. He is a multifaceted person who uses his intellect and the blessings given to him by God to excel in various areas. He is both a teacher and a student, always learning and teaching, and is able to master any subject he comes across.

He is a selfless social activist and motivational speaker who has overcome struggles and failures to become a successful and enthusiastic individual with a rich life experience.

In addition to his work with the Bhagavad Gita, he is also an efficient Tarot card reader, Astro-Vastu consultant, and a talented singer and composer. He has sung the entire Ram Charita Manas and Bhagavad Gita in his own compositions, and has sung the phrase "Lokah Samastha Sukhino Bhavantu" in 50 different languages. He is currently working on a detailed and scientific study of Vedas, Upanishads, Puranas, and the Bhagavad Gita. He has also composed and sung the Hanuman Chalisa and Gayatri Mantra in 108 and 1008 different compositions, respectively.

Awards - Four Times Guinness World Records, Winner of Mahatma Gandhi Vishwa Shanti Puraskar, Mahatma Gandhi Global Peace Ambassador, Kashi Ratna Award, Dr. APJ Abdul Kalam Motivational Person of the Year 2017, Mother Teresa Award, Indira Gandhi Priyadarshini Award, Bharat Vikas Ratna Award, Udyog Ratna Award, Vigyan Prasar Award, Poorvanchal Ratn Samman.

Preface

Change can be difficult, and it often requires us to step out of our comfort zones and take risks. This book is designed to inspire and motivate you to take action and make the changes you desire.

"Motivational Quotes for Change: Harnessing the Power of Words" is a collection of powerful quotes and practical strategies for making change. Each chapter delves into a different aspect of change, from understanding motivation and building resilience to making connections and taking action. The book also includes exercises and activities to help you put the concepts into practice.

The power of words is immense, and the quotes included in this book have been carefully selected to inspire and motivate you to take action. They serve as a reminder that change is possible and that with the right mindset and tools, you can achieve your goals.

Whether you're looking to make a change in your personal or professional life, this book is for you. It's a guide to help you navigate the process of change and achieve success.

We hope that this book will serve as a source of inspiration and motivation as you take steps towards achieving your goals. We wish you all the best in your journey towards change.

I

The Power of Words - Exploring the Power of Words and their ability to Motivate and Inspire

Words have the power to shape our thoughts, influence our emotions, and ultimately guide our actions. They can inspire us to greatness and motivate us to overcome seemingly impossible obstacles. In this chapter, we will explore the power of words and how they can be used to create positive change in our lives.

One of the most powerful ways that words can motivate

and inspire is through the use of motivational quotes. These short, memorable phrases can provide a much-needed boost of inspiration when we are feeling down or uncertain. They can serve as a reminder of our goals and aspirations, and help us to focus on what is truly important in life.

The power of words can also be seen in the way they can be used to create a sense of community and belonging. Words can bring people together, unite them in a common cause, and help to create a sense of shared purpose. This is why speeches and rallies are such powerful tools for social change. Through the use of words, leaders can inspire others to take action and make a positive impact in the world.

Words can also have a powerful impact on our emotions. They can be used to evoke feelings of hope, joy, and optimism, or to create feelings of fear, anger, and despair. This is why it is important to be mindful of the words we use and the impact they may have on others. By choosing our words carefully, we can help to create a more positive and uplifting environment for ourselves and those around us.

The power of words is undeniable. They have the ability to motivate and inspire, bring people together, and shape our thoughts and emotions. By harnessing the power of words, we can create positive change in our lives and the world around us. Remember that every words you speak or write has a power to change somebody's life, so be careful and choose your words wisely.

"The more you know yourself, the less you are prone to making ethical mistakes."

- J.C. Watts

ஐ

II

Understanding Change - Examining how Change Works and How to Embrace It

Change is an inevitable part of life, but it can be difficult to accept and navigate. In this chapter, we will examine how change works and how to embrace it in order to create positive growth and development in our lives.

First, it is important to understand that change is a process, not a single event. It often involves a series of small steps, rather than a sudden transformation. This can make it easier to accept and adapt to change, as it allows us to focus on the present and take things one step at a time.

Another key aspect of change is that it is often accompanied by uncertainty and discomfort. It can be difficult to let go of the familiar and embrace something new, but it is important to remember that change can lead to growth and new opportunities. By being open to change and embracing it, we can discover new perspectives and experiences that we may not have otherwise encountered.

To embrace change, it is also important to have a growth mindset. This means approaching change with a willingness to learn and adapt, rather than fearing it or resisting it. By embracing a growth mindset, we can approach change with curiosity and a positive attitude, which can make it easier to navigate and ultimately lead to personal growth.

Additionally, it's important to set a clear goal, plan and take action to achieve it. Break it down into smaller steps and focus on the present, this way you will be able to stay on track and measure your progress. Having a clear goal in mind and a plan to achieve it can help to give you a sense of direction and purpose during times of change.

Finally, it's important to have a support system and to surround yourself with people who will encourage and support you during times of change. This can include friends, family, mentors, or a therapist. They can provide a sounding board for your thoughts and feelings, and offer guidance and support as you navigate the changes in your life.

Change can be difficult to accept and navigate, but by

understanding how it works and embracing it, we can create positive growth and development in our lives. By embracing a growth mindset, setting a clear goal and having a support system, we can navigate change and ultimately come out stronger on the other side.

"The only way to do great work is to love what you do. If you haven't found it yet, keep looking."

- Steve Jobs

ఐ

III

Overcoming Obstacles - Strategies for Recognizing and Overcoming Obstacles

Obstacles are an inevitable part of life, but they do not have to hold us back from achieving our goals. In this chapter, we will explore strategies for recognizing and overcoming obstacles that may be standing in the way of our success.

The first step in overcoming obstacles is recognizing them. This may seem simple, but it can be easy to overlook or minimize the challenges that we are facing. By being honest with ourselves about the obstacles that we are facing, we can better understand what we need to do to overcome them.

Once we have recognized the obstacles that we are facing, it is important to develop a plan for overcoming them. This may involve breaking the obstacle down into smaller, more manageable parts, or seeking help from others. It is also important to be flexible and open to new solutions, as what worked in the past may not work in the current situation.

Another key strategy for overcoming obstacles is to focus on what we can control, rather than what we cannot control. It is easy to get caught up in the things that are out of our control, but this will only lead to feelings of helplessness and frustration. Instead, focus on the things that you can control, such as your actions and reactions, and take steps to make progress towards your goals.

It's also important to maintain a positive attitude and not to give up too soon. Obstacles can be overwhelming, but it's important to remind yourself that every challenge is an opportunity to grow and learn. Keeping a positive attitude can help to keep you motivated and focused on the ultimate goal, even when things get tough.

Obstacles are an inevitable part of life, but they do not have to hold us back from achieving our goals. By recognizing and developing a plan to overcome obstacles, focusing on what we can control, and maintaining a positive attitude, we can move through these challenges and come out stronger on the other side.

"When one door of happiness closes, another opens, but often we look so long at the closed door that we do not see the one that has been opened for us."

- Helen Keller

ꕤ

IV

Reframing Your Thinking - Learning to Reframe Your Thinking to Create Positive Outcomes

Our thoughts and perspectives can have a powerful impact on the outcomes of our lives. In this chapter, we will explore the concept of reframing our thinking, and how it can be used to create positive outcomes.

Reframing is the process of looking at a situation or problem from a different perspective, in order to gain a different understanding or insight. It involves reinterpreting events, emotions, and thoughts in a more positive or constructive way.

For example, instead of looking at a failure as a setback, reframing it as an opportunity to learn and grow can change the way we feel about it and motivate us to move forward. Similarly, instead of looking at an obstacle as an insurmountable barrier, reframing it as a challenge to be overcome can change the way we approach it and increase our chances of success.

Another important aspect of reframing is to focus on what we can control, rather than what we cannot control. By focusing on the things that we can control, we can take action to improve the situation and create positive outcomes.

Additionally, it's important to change the language you use to talk to yourself. Negative self-talk can have a detrimental effect on our mental and emotional well-being. Instead of using negative words or phrases, try to use more positive and empowering language. This can help to shift your mindset and improve your outlook on life.

Reframing our thinking can be a powerful tool for creating positive outcomes in our lives. By looking at situations and problems from a different perspective, focusing on what we can control, and using positive language, we can change the way we think and feel about the challenges we face, and ultimately increase our chances of success.

"Happiness is not something ready made. It comes from your own actions."

- Dalai Lama

ॐ

V

Developing Positive Habits - Learning How to Develop Positive Habits to Foster Change

Habits play a crucial role in shaping our daily lives and ultimately determining the outcome of our overall well-being. In this chapter, we will explore the process of developing positive habits and how they can be used to foster change in our lives.

The first step in developing positive habits is to identify the specific behaviors or actions that you want to change. This could be something as simple as drinking more water, or as complex as developing a consistent exercise routine.

Once you have identified the habit you want to change, it's important to set a clear and specific goal.

Next, it's important to create a plan of action. Break down the habit into smaller and manageable steps, and set a schedule for when you will perform the habit. This can help to make the habit more manageable and achievable.

Another important aspect of developing positive habits is to track your progress. Keeping a record of your progress can help you to stay motivated and on track. It can also help you to identify any obstacles that may be standing in your way and find ways to overcome them.

It's also important to be patient and persistent. Changing a habit takes time and effort, and it's important to remember that progress is rarely linear. There will be days when you slip up or don't make progress, but it's important to not get discouraged and keep working towards your goal.

Developing positive habits is a powerful tool for fostering change in our lives. By identifying specific behaviors or actions, setting a clear and specific goal, creating a plan of action, tracking progress, being patient and persistent, we can develop positive habits that can help us to achieve our goals and improve our overall well-being.

"The greatest glory in living lies not in never falling, but in rising every time we fall."

- Nelson Mandela

ꕥ

VI

Building Resilience - Strategies for Building Resilience and Staying Motivated

Resilience is the ability to bounce back from adversity and stay motivated in the face of challenges. In this chapter, we will explore strategies for building resilience and staying motivated.

The first step in building resilience is to understand the connection between your thoughts, emotions, and actions. When we are faced with a difficult situation, our thoughts and emotions can easily spiral out of control, leading to feelings of helplessness and defeat. By learning to recognize and challenge negative thoughts, we can change the way we feel about a situation and take control of our actions.

Another important aspect of building resilience is developing a support system. This could include friends, family, or a therapist. Having a support system can provide a sounding board for your thoughts and emotions and help you to stay motivated.

It's also important to practice self-care. This includes things like exercise, healthy eating, and getting enough sleep. When we take care of our physical and emotional well-being, we are better equipped to handle stress and challenges.

Additionally, it's crucial to focus on the present moment and not dwelling on the past or worrying about the future. Mindfulness practices like meditation, journaling, and yoga, can help to bring focus to the present moment and reduce feelings of anxiety and stress.

Building resilience is essential for staying motivated in the face of challenges. By understanding the connection between our thoughts, emotions, and actions, developing a support system, practicing self-care, and focusing on the present moment, we can build resilience and stay motivated on our journey towards achieving our goals.

"The best way to predict your future is to create it."

- Abraham Lincoln

ထ

VII

Developing Self-Compassion - Practicing Self-Compassion and Understanding its Importance

Self-compassion is the ability to be kind and understanding towards oneself, especially during difficult times. In this chapter, we will explore the concept of self-compassion, and how it can be practiced and developed.

Self-compassion includes three key elements: self-kindness, common humanity, and mindfulness. Self-kindness refers to being gentle and understanding with oneself, rather than harsh and critical. Common humanity means understanding that suffering and imperfection is a part of the human experience and not something unique to oneself. Mindfulness is about being present and aware of one's thoughts and feelings in a non-judgmental way.

One way to practice self-compassion is to talk to yourself in a kind and understanding way, as you would to a friend. This means avoiding self-criticism and instead, offering yourself words of encouragement and support.

Another way to practice self-compassion is through mindfulness meditation, which can help to increase awareness of one's thoughts and feelings, and reduce negative self-talk.

It's also important to remind oneself that perfection is not achievable or necessary, and to give oneself permission to make mistakes and be imperfect. Remembering that we all have moments of suffering and struggles can also help to foster a sense of common humanity and reduce feelings of isolation.

Incorporating self-compassionate practices into your daily routine can have a significant impact on mental and emotional well-being. Research has shown that self-compassion is associated with increased emotional regulation, greater psychological well-being, and improved relationships.

Developing self-compassion is crucial for our overall well-being. By practicing self-kindness, understanding our common humanity, and being mindful, we can reduce negative self-talk, increase our ability to handle difficult situations and improve our mental and emotional well-being. Incorporating self-compassionate practices into your daily routine can have a significant impact on our overall well-being and help us to be more kind and understanding towards ourselves and others.

"The only limit to our realization of tomorrow will be our doubts of today."

- Franklin D. Roosevelt

ഗ

VIII

Understanding Your Motivation - Examining Your Motivation and How to Use it to Your Advantage

Motivation is the driving force that drives us to achieve our goals and aspirations. In this chapter, we will explore the concept of motivation and how to use it to your advantage.

To understand your motivation, it's important to first identify what it is that drives you. This could be a desire for success, the feeling of accomplishment, or the sense of purpose that comes with achieving a goal. Once you have identified your motivation, you can use it to set specific and achievable goals.

Another way to use your motivation to your advantage is by creating a plan of action. Break down your goal into smaller and manageable steps, and set a schedule for when you will work towards achieving it. This can help to make your goal more achievable and increase your chances of success.

It's also important to stay motivated by reminding yourself of the reasons why you started, and the benefits that will come with achieving your goal. Keeping a journal, or visualizing your end goal, can help to keep you motivated when things get tough.

Additionally, it's crucial to surround yourself with people who will support and encourage you. The support and encouragement of others can help to keep you motivated and on track.

It's also important to create a plan of action and establish a routine. Having a clear plan and routine can help to keep you motivated and on track to achieving your goals. It's also important to break down your goals into smaller, manageable tasks, and schedule time for working on them.

Another important aspect of understanding your motivation is to stay self-aware and monitor your progress. Reflecting on your progress and identifying any obstacles that may be standing in your way can help you to stay motivated and adjust your plan of action as needed.

It's essential to have a positive mindset and believe in

yourself. Having a positive attitude and believing in your ability to achieve your goals can help to keep you motivated and overcome any obstacles that may arise.

Extrinsic motivation, on the other hand, comes from external factors such as rewards or recognition. Both types of motivation can be effective, but it's important to find a balance and ensure that you are motivated by both internal and external factors.

It's also important to understand the role of self-talk in motivation. Our internal dialogue can have a powerful effect on our motivation levels. Negative self-talk can decrease motivation, while positive self-talk can increase it. By recognizing and changing negative self-talk to positive one we can increase our motivation.

One way to increase motivation is to break down large goals into smaller, more manageable tasks. This can make the goal feel less daunting and more achievable. Additionally, setting clear and specific goals, and creating a plan of action can also increase motivation.

Understanding your motivation is essential for achieving your goals and living a fulfilling life. By identifying your values and goals, recognizing the different types of motivation, managing self-talk, breaking down large goals into smaller tasks, and setting clear and specific goals, we can use our motivation to our advantage and achieve our desired outcome.

"Positive anything is better than negative nothing."

- Elbert Hubbard

ꕤ

IX

Inspirational Quotes - Exploring Inspirational Quotes and Their Power

Inspirational quotes have the power to motivate, inspire, and encourage us. In this chapter, we will explore the power of inspirational quotes and how they can be used to achieve our goals and improve our lives.

Inspirational quotes can help to shift our mindset and perspective. They can provide a sense of hope and inspiration in difficult times, and remind us of our potential and capabilities. They can also serve as a source of wisdom and guidance, helping us to navigate the challenges of life.

One way to use inspirational quotes is to write them down and place them in a visible location, such as on a bulletin board or in a journal. This allows us to see the quote daily and be reminded of its message.

Another way to use inspirational quotes is to use them as a source of motivation for specific goals or challenges. For example, if you're facing a difficult task, finding a quote that relates to perseverance and determination can be a powerful motivator.

Additionally, reading or listening to inspirational quotes regularly can help to cultivate a positive and optimistic mindset. This can be especially helpful in times of stress and uncertainty.

Inspirational quotes have the power to motivate, inspire, and encourage us. By using them as a source of wisdom, guidance, and motivation, we can improve our mindset, achieve our goals and navigate the challenges of life.

"Believe in yourself and all that you are. Know that there is something inside you that is greater than any obstacle."

ꙮ

X

Making Connections - Understanding the Importance of Making Connections and Building Relationships

Making connections and building relationships is an essential aspect of personal and professional growth. In this chapter, we will explore the importance of making connections and building relationships, and how to do so effectively.

Having a strong network of connections can provide a variety of benefits such as access to new opportunities, resources, and support. Building relationships with people who have similar interests or goals can also provide a sense of community and belonging.

One effective way to make connections is by actively seeking out new opportunities to meet people. This can include joining clubs or organizations, attending networking events, or reaching out to people in your field of interest.

Another important aspect of making connections is building trust and developing strong relationships. This can be done by being reliable, open and honest in your interactions, and actively listening to others.

It's also important to diversify your connections. This means connecting with people from different backgrounds, cultures, and industries. Diversifying your connections can expose you to new perspectives and ideas, and help you to grow both personally and professionally.

Making connections and building relationships is essential for personal and professional growth. By actively seeking out new opportunities to meet people, building trust, and diversifying your connections, you can expand your network and gain access to new opportunities, resources, and support.

ꕥ

"Success is not final, failure is not fatal: it is the courage to continue that counts."

XI

Taking Action - Creating an Action Plan and Taking Steps Towards Change

One of the most important aspects of achieving change is taking action. In this chapter, we will explore the process of creating an action plan and taking steps towards change.

The first step in taking action is to set specific and measurable goals. This means breaking down your overall goal into smaller, more manageable steps and setting a deadline for when you want to achieve them. Having specific and measurable goals will help to make the process of change more manageable and increase your chances of success.

The next step is to create an action plan. This is a detailed roadmap that outlines the steps you will take to achieve your goals. Your action plan should include tasks, deadlines, and any resources you will need to complete them.

Once you have set your goals and created an action plan, it's time to take action. This means putting your plan into action and taking the necessary steps to achieve your goals. It's important to remember that change takes time and that progress may not always be linear.

Another important aspect of taking action is to be consistent and persistent. This means staying committed to your goals and continuing to take action even when things get difficult.

Taking action is a crucial step in achieving change. By setting specific and measurable goals, creating an action plan, and taking consistent and persistent action, you can increase your chances of success.

Other Books Of The Author

1. The Moments When I Met God
2. Kashiyile Theertha Pathangal
3. GURU GYAN VANI
4. Abhiprerak Gita
5. ASSI SE JAIN GHAT TAK
6. Hopelessness of Arjuna
7. The Soul and It's True Nature
8. Sense of Action (Karma)
9. Action through Wisdom
10. Action through Wisdom
11. THEORY AND PRACTICAL OF EVERY ACTION
12. LOGICAL UNDERSTANDING OF THE SUPREME
13. THE IMPERISHABLE SUPREME
14. Yatra Nishadraj se Hanuman Ghat Tak
15. Yatra Karnatak Ghat se Raja Ghat Tak
16. Yatra Pandey Ghat se Prayagraj Ghat Tak
17. Yatra Ranjendra Prasad Ghat se Dattatreya Ghat Tak
18. YaatraSindhiya Ghat se Gwaliar Ghat Tak
19. Yatra Mangala Gauri Ghat se Hanuman Gadhi Ghat Tak
20. Yatra Gaay Ghat Se Nishad Ghat Tak
21. MAA GANGA, GHATEN EVM UTSAV
22. Ganga Arti Dev Deepavali evam Any Utsav
23. Potentials of Digitalized India
24. VEDIC CONSCIOUSNESS
25. A Brief Introduction to Vedic Science
26. Kashi ke Barah Jyotirling
27. IMPACT OF MOTIVATION
28. Let's have a Milky Way Journey
29. Color Therapy in a Nutshell

30. Rigveda in a Nutshell
31. Yajurveda in a Nutshell
32. Samveda in a Nutshell
33. Atharva Veda in a Nutshell
34. Ayushman Bhava - Ayurveda
35. Srimad Bhagavad Gita and Upanishad Connection
36. Srimad Bhagavad Gita - an attempt to summarize each chapter.
37. Facts and Impact of Nakshatra
38. Astro Gems - NAVARATNA
39. Ekadashi - A Concise Overview
40. A Concise View of Hanuman Chalisa
41. Inspirational Gita
42. Nakshatraranyam
43. Summary of 18 Mahapuranas
44. Synopsis of 18 Upa Puranas
45. Rigvediya Upanishads
46. Shukla Yajurvediya Upanishads
47. Krishna Yajurvediya Upanishads
48. Samavediya Upanishads
49. Atharvavediya Upanishads
50. The Seven Great Sages
51. From Rocket Scientist to President Dr. APJ Abdul Kalam
52. The Visionary's Voice - Quotes of Dr. APJ Abdul Kalam
53. The Wisdom of Swami Vivekananda: Insights and Inspiration from a Legendary Spiritual Teacher
54. Ayurvedic Remedies from the Garden
55. Sages and Seers
56. Rising Strong – Motivational Stories of Women
57. Beyond Flames -Mystery stories of Funeral Ghat Manikarnika
58. The Origins of Tulsi: A Look at the Mythological Roots of the Plant"

59. The Holistic Cow: A Look at the Physical, Spiritual, and Cultural Importance of Cows in India
60. Arts of Healing
61. Exploring the Divine
62. Understanding Five Elements
63. The Etymology of Ram
64. Symbols of India
65. Voice of Change (About Speeches of Great Men)
66. She Speaks (About Speeches of Great Women)
67. Patriotism on Celluloid – Brief About Patriotic Films
68. The Music of Motivation: A Brief Guide to Inspirational Film Songs
69. **Unlocking the Secrets of the Dashopanishads**
70. A Cultural Mosaic
71. Ancient Traditions, Modern Minds
72. Ecos of Ancient Wisdom
73. Beneath the Surface
74. From Temples to Ashrams
75. Sages of the Subcontinent
76. The Art of Healling (Ayurveda, Yoga & Naturopathy)
77. Indian Kitchen
78. The Festivals of India
79. The Indian Epics Retold
80. The Power of Mantras
81. The Indian River Ganges
82. The Indian Architecture
83. Rites of Passage
84. The Indian Silk Road
85. The Indian Literature
86. The Indian Villages
87. The Indian Folks & Crafts
88. The Way of Buddha
89. The Ramayan of Tulsidas

90. Astrological Remedies
91. The Secret Power of Motivation
92. Secret of Developing your Inner Strength
93. The Secret Path to Motivation
94. The Art and Secret of Positive Thinking
95. The Secrets of Practicing Ethical Living
96. Indian Art and Painting
97. The Indian Herbalism
98. Bharatanatyam to Kathak
99. Exploring India's Astrological Remedies
100. The Indian Festival of Flowers
101. Indian Handicrafts
102. The Splashes of Joy – India's Colour Festival

CONTACT

DR. JAGADEESH PILLAI

PhD in Vedic Science

Four Times Guinness World Record Holder

Winner of Mahatma Gandhi Vishwa Shanti Puraskar and
Global Peace Ambassador

Gemology, Astro & Vastu Consultant - Spiritual Counselor

Consultant for designing World Record Ideas

Efficient Tarot Card Reader

9839093003

myrichindia@gmail.com

drjagadeeshpillai@facebook

drjagadeeshpillai@instagram

jagadeeshpillai@youtube

www. JAGADEESHPILLAI.com

|| LOKAHA SAMASTHAHA SUKHINO BHAVANTU ||

9 798889 519607

Printed by Libri Plureos GmbH in Hamburg,
Germany